A NOTE FROM MOM

When Hays was first diagnosed with Type One Diabetes, there were so many unknowns. It was a new—and seemingly scary—journey for our family. We had so much support rally around us, join us in the education classes, and ask how they could help.

Since that initial timeframe, our support system has only grown. Between family, friends, medical staff, and school personnel, our boy is loved and known. He is an advocate for himself as well.

This book began taking shape soon after his diagnosis, but it has developed and changed as we have grown and learned. While there are many different ways to manage life with Type One, we hope this insight will prove to be helpful for you in whatever your capacity and connection is.

Thank you for reading and being part of Hays' Type One-derful Journey.

Jolie Gray, mom
jolie.gray@thegraymatters.com

MANY THANKS

This book is dedicated to my friends, family, and medical team that have helped me. Thank you!

HaysPlays.com

ISBN 978-1-7340647-0-4

HAYS'
TYPE ONE-DERFUL
JOURNEY

Written and Illustrated by

Hays Gray

Hi, I'm Hays.
I was diagnosed with Type One Diabetes when I was four.

Before my diagnosis, I was drinking a lot of water and going to the bathroom more than usual. My mom was getting worried, so we went to the doctor. The nurse pricked my finger and I went to the bathroom in a cup.

They told us to go to the hospital. The hospital workers told me that I had Type One Diabetes and that my body wasn't producing insulin correctly. If you have Type Two Diabetes, your body is producing insulin, but it can't use it right. T-Paw, my mom's dad, has Type Two.

I stayed in the hospital for three days. I got to order off the menu for breakfast, lunch, and dinner, and my mom and dad practiced counting my carbs. In the hospital, I had to do sugar checks with the grown-up poker that hurt. But they got me a kid one that you could move to make it hurt less. Then I had to do insulin. First I had syringes with a longer needle and then I got a pen. That is for my fast-acting insulin I get every time I eat. I also have to have a shot that lasts all day and night that is long-acting insulin.

I got a bear in the hospital named Rufus; he has Type One just like me. We got him some clothes from Build-A-Bear. We saw a cool Aggie jersey that I wanted for him, but I had to save up my money for next time. Rufus has patches so I can practice finger pokes and injection spots in his legs, arms, tummy, and hiney.

Sometimes my sugar gets low or high. It might be just a little high or a little low. If my sugar is high, I need insulin. If I'm low, I might get to have chocolate or candy. When I drink water, it helps my insulin work. I can still celebrate and enjoy parties with my friends, too.

cheese

pepperonis †urkey

Beef jerky

pickles

-almonds/

I like when I get to have free snacks. Free snacks are snacks with few or no carbs that don't need much, if any, insulin, like turkey, cheese, almonds, pickles, beef jerky, and pepperoni. I can have a free snack pretty much anytime I want to.

I wanted to write a book to tell other kids that when you have Type One Diabetes you will go to the hospital and get some really cool stuff to take care of your body. As you grow and learn, sometimes what you use for your care will change.

Sometimes I feel different than my friends because they don't have Type One Diabetes, but Type One doesn't stop me from doing anything that my friends do. I can do art. I can run around and play outside. I read books. I can do anything that's at school. I still play sports; I'm a great soccer player, and I play baseball, too. I like to sled and ski when it's snowy.

It has been four years since I was diagnosed with Type One Diabetes (and I saved up enough money for that jersey for Rufus). Now I have gotten used to the steps I have to take with Type One.

I don't feel so different from my friends anymore. This summer, I went to Camp Bluebonnet with other kids who have been diagnosed with Type One like me.

me ↓

Dexcom ↘

Before second grade, I got a Dexcom G6. While I was at camp, I got to see lots of technology other kids were using. I was excited to get my Dexcom and a little bit nervous. A Dexcom is a device that helps us know what my sugar is without having to do finger pokes. I wear it on my legs. We change it every ten days. My Dexcom talks to my phone; my phone beeps when I am high or low and also alerts my mom and dad. We don't rely on my Dexcom fully; sometimes we still have to poke my finger and I always listen to my body.

My Type One Diabetes team is a group of doctors, nurses, and diabetes educators that help my mom and dad keep me safe. I go to a special doctor called an endocrinologist; I also see a nurse practitioner. We go to the endo's office every ninety days. At each appointment, we talk to my team; tell them what we have been doing; and ask them if we need to make any changes. After my appointment, we usually go to Target, the Lego Store, or Build-A-Bear. I get something from one of those stores for me to play with or for my Type One bear, Rufus.

If you were just diagnosed with Type One Diabetes and you are hearing this book, don't be afraid. It is a little scary at first, but you will get used to it like I did. Count your carbs and make sure you follow your endo's instructions. Be brave and help your family know if there is something wrong.

I'm Hays, and thanks for reading!
Be sure to check out my YouTube Channel - Hays Plays!

HaysPlays.com
instagram.com/HaysPlays
facebook.com/HaysPlays

ABOUT THE AUTHOR

Hays Gray is sharing part of his story in his debut book. He began writing it soon after his diagnosis in 2015 (age 4) and sent to publish just before his 9th birthday. He has a passion for helping others and making sure they don't feel alone in their diagnosis.

He loves Legos, the Aggies, baseball, basketball, and adventures with his family. He enjoys sharing on his YouTube channel, Hays Plays. Explode a watermelon or learn how to apply a Dexcom sensor—he does it all!

He has been an ambassador for his local JDRF chapter and is hopeful he will have the opportunity to participate in Children's Congress through JDRF as well. He enjoys fundraising for the OneWalk and participating in walk day events.

He knows that even though he has a diagnosis of Type One Diabetes he is so much more than just that and can do anything he puts his mind to!

www.ingramcontent.com/pod-product-compliance
Lightning Source LLC
Chambersburg PA
CBHW042021090426

42811CB00016B/1698